You smell

and taste and feel and see and hear

Mary Murphy

I taste cold, creamy milk.

I feel a scritchy, scratchy comb.

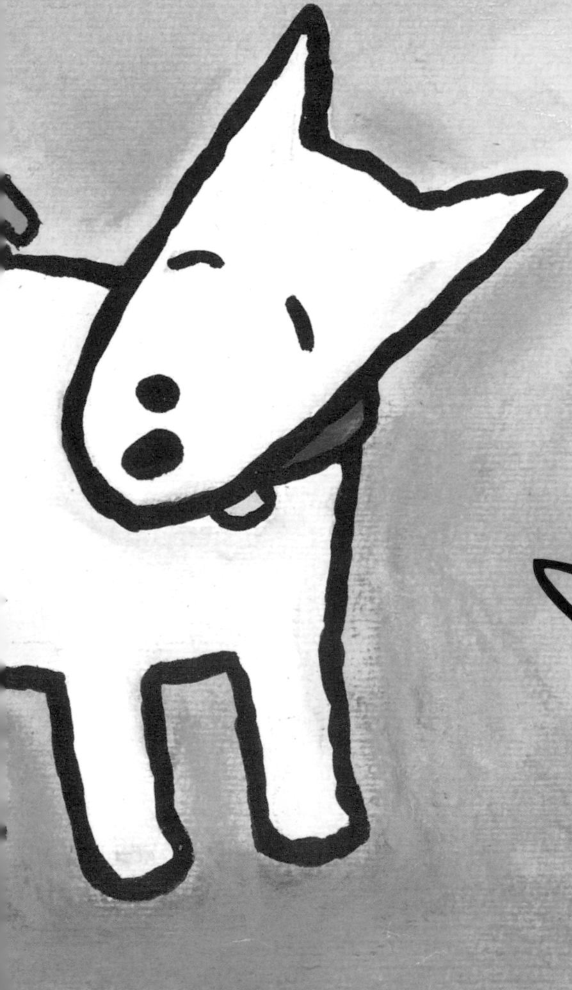

I hear my bricks CRASH!

I taste salty snacks.

I hear my friend
on the telephone.

We hear the leaves rustle

quietly in the breeze.

I feel the
rain fall.

I see me.

Rowf!

I see a cat.

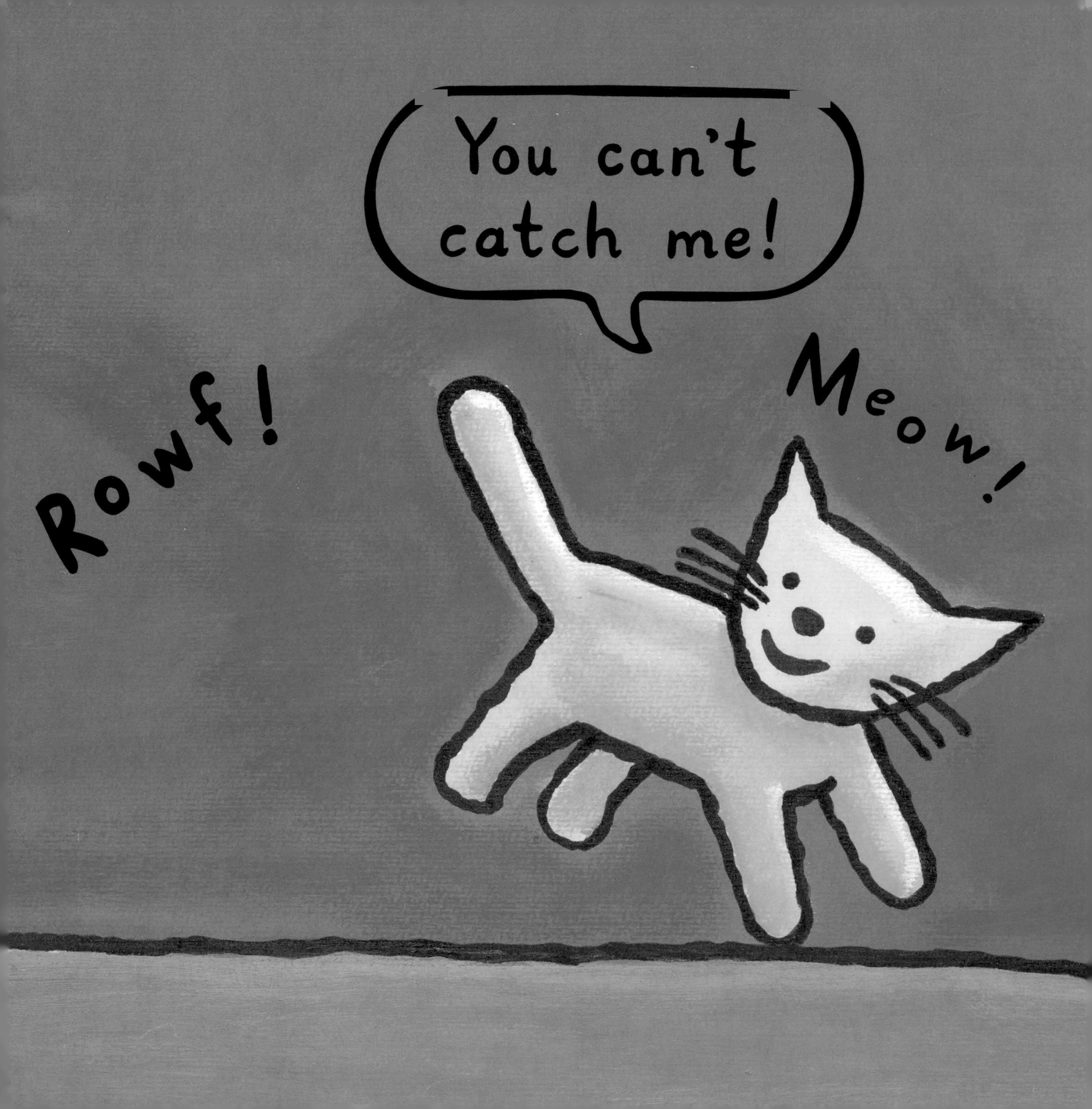
You can't catch me!
Rowf!
Meow!

I smell a muddy puddle.
It feels lovely!

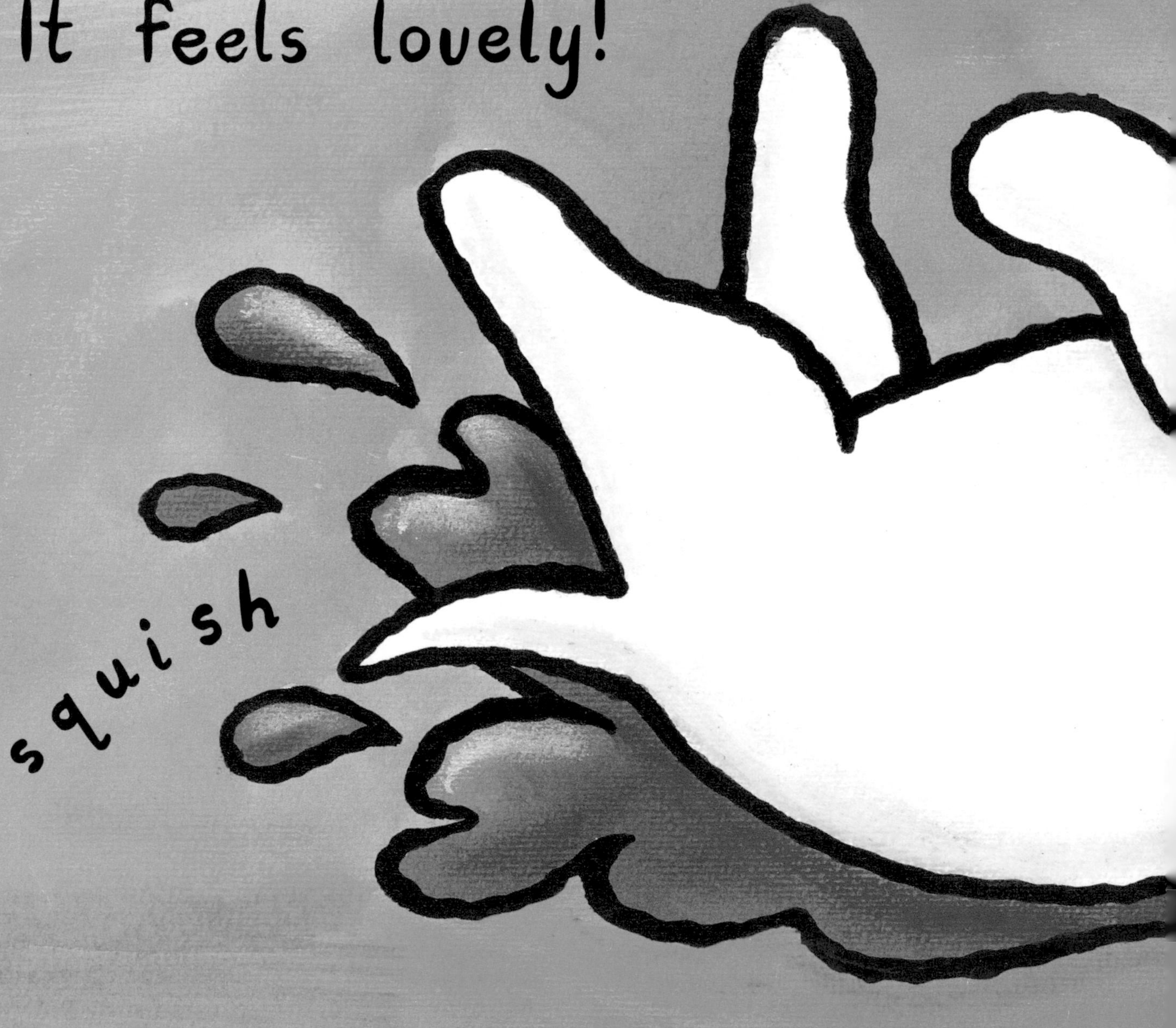

I see the

moon far away.

I smell dinner.
Time to go in!

Yuk!

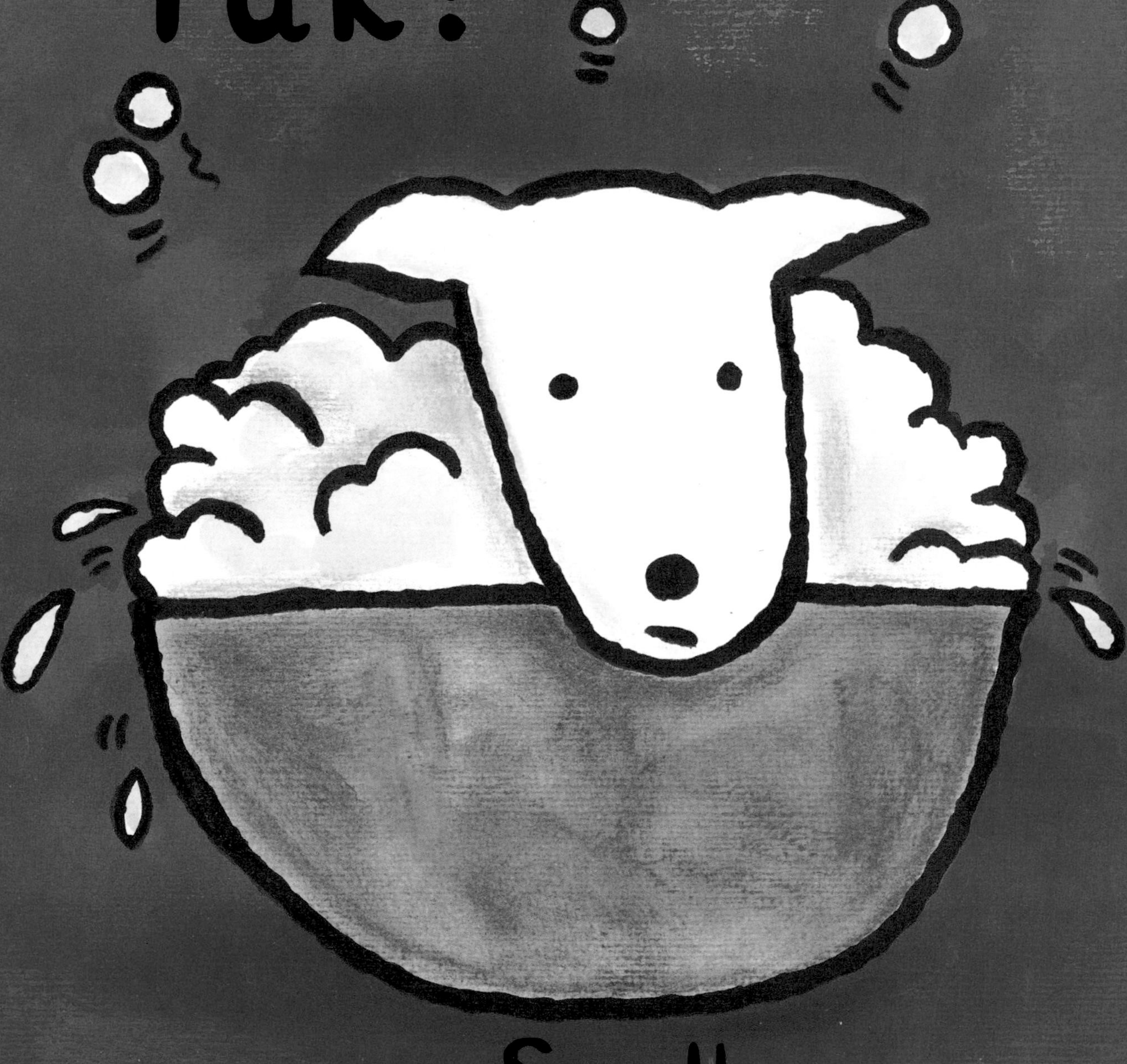

Smelly soap.

I taste sweet hot chocolate.

I feel a

big,

warm hug.